English Olympiad

Book 7

© **B. Jain Publishers (P) Ltd.** All rights reserved. No part of this book may be reproduced, stored in a retrieval system or transmitted, in any form or by any means, mechanical, photocopying, recording or otherwise, without any prior written permission of the publisher.

Published by Kuldeep Jain for B. Jain Publishers (P) Ltd., D-157, Sector 63, Noida - 201307, U.P.

Registered office: 1921/10, Chuna Mandi, Paharganj, New Delhi-110055

Printed in India at Narain Printers & Binder, Noida

Preface

English Olympiad Book 7 has been carefully written, designed and brought to fruition in the hope that it carries all necessary elements that make each exercise a learning experience for children, their teachers and parents. It also ensures gradual progression from English Olympiad Book 6.

'Learning by doing' - the ethos behind introducing Olympiads is an effort to achieve perfection. In this spirit, we have followed a systematic pattern, inclusive of the scientific method and child-centric approach, wherein each concept has been explained again (as understood that it was done as part of grammar lessons). Therefore, revisions here leave enough room to substantiate upon experiential learning that help students to deliver better.

In the end, we have also provided five test papers that carry a diverse set of questions. It will help children test themselves amidst all concepts put together in random order, which will bring greater degree of clarity and thought.

Salient Features

- Multiple choice questions
- Use of necessary illustrations to make learning simpler
- Model test papers in the end to make a wholesome assessment
- Inclusion of almost all aspects of English Olympiad exams

We wish all readers of **English Olympiad Book-7** a joyful experience.

CONTENTS

1. Synonyms 5
2. Antonyms 8
3. Analogies and Spellings 11
4. One word substitutions, Proverbs, Facts and Opinion 13
5. Sentences and Sentence Sequencing 17
6. Nouns and Pronouns 20
7. Verbs and Phrasal Verbs 24
8. Adverbs and Adjectives 27
9. Articles and Prepositions 30
10. Conjunctions and Punctuations 33
11. Tenses 36
12. Voices and Narration 40
13. Short Composition 45
14. Sequences - Stories, Events and Snippets 48
15. Comprehension 51
16. Spoken and Written Expression 54
    Model Test Paper-1 56
    Model Test Paper-2 60
    Model Test Paper-3 64
    Model Test Paper-4 68
    Model Test Paper-5 72

Answer Key 76

SYNONYMS

EXERCISE 1

Mark the correct synonyms for the words given below.

1. **Amazing**
   a) Wonderful   b) Ordinary   c) Beautiful   d) Joyous

2. **Abrupt**
   a) Methodological   b) Hurried   c) Slow   d) Unexpected

3. **Accept**
   a) Appoint   b) Agree   c) Refuse   d) Reject

4. **Accomplish**
   a) Achieve   b) Declare   c) Adequate   d) Compel

5. **Beautiful**
   a) Dull   b) Ugly   c) Attractive   d) Shy

6. **Brave**
   a) Unhappy   b) Courageous   c) Handsome   d) Coward

7. **Bright**
   a) Shiny   b) Dull   c) Interesting   d) Boring

8. **Climax**
   a) Foundation   b) Upgrade   c) Abnormal   d) High point

9. **Angry**
   a) Happy   b) Sad   c) Furious   d) Poor

10. **Conceal**
    a) Rough   b) Hide   c) Seen   d) Visible

11. **Comprehend**
    a) Known   b) Quick   c) Eligible   d) Understand

12. **Calm**
    a) Listen   b) Great   c) Angry   d) Composed

13. **Confident**
    a) Invincible   b) Wise   c) Modern   d) Assured

14. **Corrupt**
    a) Dishonest   b) Reliable   c) Principled   d) Wicked

15. **Dangerous**
    a) Horror   b) Safe   c) Risky   d) Unseen

16. **Distant**
    a) Far   b) Removed   c) Separate   d) Intelligent

17. **Demolish**
    a) Built   b) Create   c) Destroy   d) Operate

18. **Diligent**
    a) Brilliant   b) Hardworking   c) Inventive   d) Progressive

19. **Explain**
    a) Elaborate   b) Brief   c) Exact   d) Fake

20. **Eager**
    a) Intelligent   b) Willing   c) Keen   d) Expert

21. **Feeble**
    a) Arrogant   b) Vain   c) Sick   d) Weak

22. **Genuine**
    a) Authentic   b) Fake   c) Active   d) Literal

23. **Venue**
    a) Agenda   b) Duration   c) Place   d) Duration

24. **Famous**
    a) Noble   b) Liberal   c) Faithful   d) Reputed

25. **Ponder**
    a) Increase   b) Expect   c) Anticipate   d) Think

26. **Prestige**
    a) Quality   b) Name   c) Wealth   d) Reputation

27. **Synopsis**
    a) Mixture   b) Puzzles   c) Summary   d) Index

28. **Remuneration**
    a) Compensation   b) Protest   c) Payment   d) Understanding

29. **Potential**
    a) Convert   b) Reluctance   c) Capacity   d) Chief

30. **Filch**
    a) Cover   b) Steal   c) Swindle   d) Prominent

31. **Rebate**
    a) Discount   b) Gift   c) Commission   d) Interest

32. **Unique**
    a) Common   b) Solo   c) Real   d) Exclusive

33. **Wrong**
    a) Correct   b) Incorrect   c) Right   d) Worth

34. **Graphic**
    a) Obscure   b) Implicit   c) Visual   d) Vague

35. **Valour**
    a) Cowardice   b) Wise   c) Courage   d) Beautiful

ANTONYMS

EXERCISE 1

Choose the correct antonym of the given words.

1. **Mortal**
   a) Immortal b) Spiritual c) Divine d) Active

2. **Busy**
   a) Engaged b) Engrossed c) Occupied d) Idle

3. **Artificial**
   a) Solid b) Natural c) Red d) Original

4. **Expand**
   a) Convert b) Congest c) Conclude d) Contract

5. **Nice**
   a) Lovely b) Unpleasant c) Decent d) Superior

6. **Obey**
   a) Agree b) Following c) Deny d) Contradicting

7. **Fraudulent**
   a) Candid b) Direct c) Genuine d) Forthright

8. **Cheap**
   a) Expensive b) Moderate c) Buy d) Economic

9. **Aware**
   a) Doubtful b) Sure c) Unaware d) Alert

10. **Shrink**
    a) Shorten b) Expand c) Spoil d) Contract

11. **Arrogant**
    a) Egotistic b) Humble c) Gentlemanly d) Cowardly

12. Victorious
a) Destroyed b) Annexed c) Vanquished d) Defeated

13. Graceful
a) Miserable b) Awkward c) Expert d) Rough

14. Rarely
a) Sometime b) Hardly c) Definitely d) Frequently

15. Adaptable
a) Yielding b) Adoptable c) Rigid d) Flexible

16. Familiar
a) Unpleasant b) Dangerous c) Weird d) Strange

17. Tangible
a) Abstract b) Solid c) Actual d) Concrete

18. Famous
a) Known b) Popular c) Disgraced d) Unknown

19. Absolute
a) Scarce b) Limited c) Faulty d) Deficient

20. Crowded
a) Busy b) Congested c) Full d) Deserted

21. Zenith
a) Top b) Bottom c) Pinnacle d) Climax

22. Doubtful
a) Fixed b) Important c) Famous d) Certain

23. Hindrance
a) Cooperation b) Aid c) Persuasion d) Agreement

24. Acquitted
a) Entrusted b) Freed c) Burdened d) Convicted

25. Suppress
a) Permit b) Stop c) Praise d) Generous

26. **Blessed**
    a) Fortunate   b) Glorified   c) Divine   d) Cursed

27. **Resolute**
    a) Impermissible   b) Cooperative   c) Bold   d) Weak

28. **Hollow**
    a) Filled   b) Substantial   c) Solid   d) Strong

29. **Valuable**
    a) Inferior   b) Invaluable   c) Average   d) Worthless

30. **Autonomy**
    a) Slavery   b) Submissiveness   c) Dependence   d) Subordination

31. **Mountain**
    a) Precipice   b) Valley   c) Plateau   d) Plain

32. **Violent**
    a) Gentle   b) Vocal   c) Harmless   d) Humble

33. **Preliminary**
    a) Second   b) Final   c) Initial   d) First

34. **Encourage**
    a) Warn   b) Disapprove   c) Dampen   d) Discourage

35. **Worry**
    a) Bother   b) Upset   c) Tense   d) Comfort

ANALOGIES AND SPELLINGS

EXERCISE 1

Tick the word that is odd.

1. **fascinating, interesting, amazing, incredible, fantastic, weird**
   a) interesting b) amazing c) incredible d) weird

2. **fair, just, objective, impartial, unbiased, prejudice**
   a) just b) impartial c) unbiased d) prejudice

3. **offering, homage, forfeit, concession, gift**
   a) concession b) gift c) offering d) forfeit

4. **maintain, brace, save, support, hold, unleash**
   a) brace b) unleash c) save d) maintain

5. **classified, demonstrate, reveal, display, manifest**
   a) display b) manifest c) reveal d) classified

6. **rich, affluent, wealthy, broke, well-off, well-to-do**
   a) affluent b) wealthy c) rich d) broke

7. **dicey, strong, stable, secure, solid, tough**
   a) stable b) secure c) dicey d) tough

8. **historic, significant, casual, considerable, landmark**
   a) casual b) considerable c) landmark d) historic

9. **ready, strengthen, aback, prepare, reinforce**
   a) prepare b) ready c) reinforce d) aback

10. **catch, banish, apprehend, arrest, detain**
    a) catch b) arrest c) detain d) banish

11. **unhappy, gay, sad, depressed, melancholy, miserable**
    a) gay b) sad c) melancholy d) miserable

12. **advent, ancient, obsolete, extinct, past**
    a) extinct   b) past   c) advent   d) obsolete

13. **fertile, fruitful, abundant, productive, dearth**
    a) dearth   b) fruitful   c) abundant   d) fertile

14. **hotel, house, dwelling, abode, domicile**
    a) dwelling   b) hotel   c) abode   d) domicile

15. **intelligent, clever, dull, brilliant, knowledgeable**
    a) clever   b) brilliant   c) intelligent   d) dull

16. **loyal, faithful, ardent, treacherous, devoted**
    a) faithful   b) treacherous   c) devoted   d) ardent

EXERCISE 2

Choose the correct spelling.

1. a) declaration   b) decalaration   c) dicleration   d) decleration
2. a) directory   b) directery   c) directry   d) daractory
3. a) advisory   b) advesory   c) avdisery   d) advisry
4. a) valuble   b) valyuble   c) valuable   d) valuabel
5. a) believe   b) belive   c) beleeve   d) bilive
6. a) beutifull   b) beautiful   c) butifull   d) beuteful
7. a) pieces   b) peezes   c) peaces   d) peeces
8. a) powetry   b) potri   c) poetry   d) potry
9. a) confedence   b) confidence   c) confidense   d) confidance
10. a) boundry   b) boundery   c) boundary   d) bondary
11. a) difitcult   b) deficulte   c) diffetcult   d) difficult
12. a) exparamint   b) ecsparement   c) experiment   d) exparamant

EXERCISE 3

Choose the word with the incorrect spelling.

1. a) beige   b) dicision   c) completely   d) recruit
2. a) abandon   b) abbreviation   c) absence   d) abcolutely
3. a) fatigue   b) flagrant   c) foreign   d) forefeit
4. a) morale   b) mortgage   c) movement   d) mermur
5. a) musician   b) mysterious   c) nagotiate   d) nervous
6. a) nuisance   b) narture   c) oases   d) oasis
7. a) recipe   b) recognition   c) recommend   d) recrut
8. a) reddest   b) reprimand   c) resined   d) restaurant
9. a) version   b) vartical   c) victim   d) vigorously
10. a) violation   b) visualse   c) volcano   d) voyage
11. a) supervisor   b) supposadly   c) threatening   d) tolerate
12. a) tongue   b) tournament   c) tragedy   d) trator

ONE WORD SUBSTITUTION, PROVERBS, FACTS AND OPINIONS

EXERCISE 1

Choose the word that best substitutes the sentence.

1. List of the topics or subjects to be considered at a meeting
   a) schedule   b) plan   c) timetable   d) agenda

2. One who possesses many talents
   a) versatile   b) exceptional   c) flexible   d) nubile

3. That which cannot be read
   a) negligible   b) incorrigible   c) illegible   d) ineligible

4. A government by nobles
   a) aristocracy   b) bureaucracy   c) democracy   d) autocracy

5. The life story of a person written by himself
   a) biology   b) drama   c) autobiography   d) novel

6. An imaginary perfect social and political system
   a) state   b) utopia   c) democracy   e) loyal

7. Animals that eat flesh
   a) vegetarian   b) herbivorous   c) omnivorous   d) carnivorous

8. A person who does not believe in the existence of God
   a) theist   b) ascetic   c) agnostic   d) atheist

9. Simplest and smallest form of plant life, present in air, water and soil; essential to life but may cause disease
   a) amoeba   b) toxin   c) virus   d) bacteria

10. Medicine that kills insects
    a) suicide   b) pesticide   c) matricide   d) homicide

11. The principle of living and acting for welfare of others.
    a) egoism	b) asceticism	c) feminism	d) altruism

12. One who lives in a foreign country
    a) immigrant	b) nationalist	c) foreigner	d) native

13. A place where monks live as a community
    a) convent	b) cathedral	d) monastery	e) diocese

14. A person who brings goods illegally into a country
    a) importer	b) fraud	c) exporter	d) smuggler

15. One who leads in any field
    a) pioneer	b) director	c) boss	d) chairman

EXERCISE 2

Complete the following proverbs and idioms

1. Better late than _____
   a) ever	b) quick	c) never	d) easy

2. _____ of all trades master of none.
   a) Peter	b) Harry	c) Tom	d) Jack

3. _____ is the best medicine.
   a) Hate	b) Laughter	c) Anger	d) Jealousy

4. A bad worker always blames his_____
   a) tools	b) fate	c) misfortune	d) equipment

5. Don't cry over spilt_____
   a) water	b) butter	c) milk	d) soup

6. When in Rome _____ as Romans do
   a) think	b) behave	c) act	d) do

7. As you sow, so shall you_____
   a) reap	b) gain	c) harvest	d) achieve

8. The cat disappeared in the dark in the twinkling of an_____.
   a) light	b) star	c) moon	d) eye

9. It's a trivial matter, don't make a mountain out of a _____.
    a) river   b) peak   c) molehill   d) rock

10. The news was like a bolt from the _____. I never expected it to happen to me.
    a) sky   b) cloud   c) blue   d) shock

11. Practice makes a man_____
    a) angry   b) busy   c) idle   d) perfect

12. Necessity is the _____
    a) sister of crime   b) mother of invention   c) a wise son   d) father of earning

EXERCISE 3

Select the most appropriate meaning from the following.

1. **When pigs fly**
    a) pigs are flying in the sky
    b) something is going to happen
    c) something that can't be changed
    d) something that will never happen

2. **A doubting Thomas**
    a) one who doesn't need evidence
    b) one who needs evidence in order to believe something
    c) one who hates others
    d) one who is doubted by others

3. **Against the clock**
    a) rushed and short on time
    b) not having clock
    c) something is not working properly
    d) the clock is spoilt

4. **A blessing in disguise**
    a) neither good nor bad
    b) something bad that became good later
    c) a person in disguise
    d) something good that isn't recognised easily

5. **All in the same boat**

   a) everybody in the boat are about to die
   b) when everyone is facing the same challenges.
   c) boat which can accommodate lots of people
   d) a task that can easily be completed

6. **Great minds think alike**

   a) great people are intelligent
   b) intelligent people think similarly
   c) doing something extra
   d) having great thinking capabilities

7. **Haste Makes Waste**

   a) doing something quickly
   b) wasting time at all times
   c) doing things in a hurry leads to poor results
   d) giving extra effort

Sentences and sentence sequencing

5

EXERCISE 1

Fill in the blanks with the correct options from the following.

1. _____ you brushed your teeth today?
   a) Do   b) Have   c) Does   d) Is

2. _____ you wake me up when the alarm beeps?
   a) Can   b) Are   c) Could   d) Will

3. _____ is the best international cricket player?
   a) Which   b) Who   c) He   d) What

4. _____ should we go in this summer vacation?
   a) Who   b) What   c) Why   d) Where

5. _____ did you buy your own car?
   a) When   b) How   c) Where   d) Who

6. _____ will you have for your dinner tonight?
   a) Where   b) How   c) What   d) Which

7. _____ you get lots of junk mails on your computer?
   a) Have   b) When   c) Can   d) Do

8. _____ you ever visited the Taj Mahal?
   a) Do   b) Have   c) Are   d) Can

9. _____ has taken my blue cap?
   a) Who   b) How   c) What   d) When

10. _____ you ever travelled in a train?
    a) Which   b) Have   c) Did   d) Which

11. _____ Sanjay meet you today?
    a) Has   b) Hasn't   c) If   d) Did

12. _____ would you like to have for dinner?
   a) Which   b) What   c) Does   d) When

13. _____ this the bag you were talking about?
   a) If   b) What   c) Which   d) Is

14. _____ she a better choice?
   a) Doesn't   b) Wouldn't   c) Shouldn't   d) Isn't

15. They played hockey last Saturday, _____ they?
   a) don't   b) didn't   c) does   d) did

16. The international student is from Germany, _____ he?
   a) isn't   b) aren't   c) wasn't   d) weren't

17. Did you feel that? That wasn't an earthquake, _____ it?
   a) is   b) were   c) was   d) are

18. Swati bought a new car, _____ she?
   a) don't   b) didn't   c) does   d) did

19. You haven't been to the new library, _____ you?
   a) have   b) hasn't   c) has   d) haven't

20. You didn't punch Rohit, _____ you?
   a) don't   b) didn't   c) does   d) did

21. Rachel wrote that letter, _____ she?
   a) don't   b) didn't   c) does   d) did

22. You can still talk, _____ you?
   a) will   b) won't   c) can't   d) can

EXERCISE 2

Rearrange the following sentences in the correct order.

1. a) the blue   b) with clouds   c) is dotted   d) sky
   a-b-c-d   d-c-a-b   a-d-c-b   c-b-a-d

2. a) those days   b) phones in   c) we had   d) no mobile
   a-b-c-d   d-c-b-a   c-d-b-a   a-d-b-c

3. a) abroad   b) every year   c) he   d) goes

    c-d-a-b   a-b-c-d   c-b-a-d   b-a-c-d

4. a) towards the   b) he walked   c) store very   d) fast

    a-b-c-d   b-a-c-d   d-c-a-b   c-a-b-d

5. a) end   b) sorted out   c) everything was   d) in the

    d-a-c-b   a-b-c-d   b-a-c-d   d-a-b-c

6. a) woman of   b) is a   c) my mother   d) few words

    d-c-b-a   c-b-a-d   a-b-c-d   b-c-d-a

7. a) from Mumbai   b) my cousin   c) us tomorrow   d) is visiting

    a-b-c-d   d-c-b-a   c-a-b-d   b-a-d-c

8. a) very carefully   b) checked   c) his patients   d) the doctor

    a-b-c-d   d-c-b-a   b-c-a-d   d-b-c-a

Nouns and Pronouns

EXERCISE 1

Pair the following with their appropriate matches.

1. **beaker**
   a) hotel   b) gym   c) bus stop   d) laboratory

2. **ampoule**
   a) timber   b) nuts   c) medicine   d) cookies

3. **knapsack**
   a) hiker   b) painter   c) carpenter   d) driver

4. **camouflage**
   a) soldier   b) artist   c) chef   d) student

5. **bells**
   a) Holi   b) Diwali   c) Dusshera   d) Christmas

6. **beads**
   a) poet   b) author   c) priest   d) engineer

7. **easel**
   a) greengrocer   b) gardener   c) cleaner   d) painter

8. **anvil**
   a) pilot   b) florist   c) cobbler   d) policeman

EXERCISE 2

Choose the correct option.

1. The board of directors refused the new proposal. (collective noun)
   a) refused   b) board of directors   c) new   d) proposal

2. What is the reason of his failure in exams? (abstract noun)
   a) reason   b) failure   c) exams   d) what

3. You cannot go out to play, first do your homework. (uncountable noun)
   a) playing   b) first   c) homework   d) outside

4. Please keep the boxes carefully. (common noun)
   a) boxes   b) please   c) keep   d) carefully

5. When their _____ is away, the servants idle around.
   a) hostess   b) host   c) master   d) stewardess

6. The _____ asked his staff to complete the proposal.
   a) emperor   b) master   c) manager   d) tailor

7. The _____ did not want to pay for the services.
   a) mute   b) thief   c) spinster   d) miser

8. He lives the life of a _____ and refuses to meet anyone.
   a) hooligan   b) hunter   c) host   d) hermit

EXERCISE 4

Fill in the correct collective noun.

1. His _____ of stamps is the best in the city.
   a) pack   b) set   c) collection   d) group

2. The _____ of dolphins leaped out of the deep ocean.
   a) pod   b) pack   c) school   d) shoal

3. The _____ of hounds ran through the dense forest.
   a) group   b) herd   c) pack   d) shoal

4. The _____ applauded with joy.
   a) group   b) visitors   c) audience   d) crowd.

5. Its not just the job of the _____.
   a) others   b) army   c) politicians   d) government

EXERCISE 5

Fill in the correct pronoun.

1. I am older than _____.
   a) it is   b) he is   c) him   d) her

2. **Nobody except _____ answered the question.**
   a) he b) she c) they d) her

3. **Usha fell off the stairs and hurt _____.**
   a) herself b) her c) him d) it

4. **The girl _____ was injured in the accident is now in the hospital.**
   a) she b) her c) whom d) who

5. **Now tell me _____ you are interested to do?**
   a) whom b) who c) which d) what

6. **More than half of _____ he says is untrue.**
   a) whose b) who c) whom d) what

7. **He _____ will not work, shall not eat.**
   a) what b) who c) whose d) whom

8. **This is a game _____ we all know.**
   a) which b) whom c) whose d) what

9. **You may buy _____ you like.**
   a) which b) what c) whose d) whom

10. **Jai, to _____ I lent some money, has asked me for some more.**
    a) whom b) what c) he d) him

11. **_____ are you saying? _____ did you speak to?**
    a) Why, what b) Who, whom c) What, whom d) What, who

12. **In _____ school was your sister taught, and by _____?**
    a) That, who b) That, whom c) Which, who d) Which, whom

13. **What he calls his property is not really _____.**
    a) theirs b) hers c) his d) he

14. **The poet prefers his own poem to _____ or _____.**
    a) you, she b) your, she c) yours, her d) yours, hers

15. **The government is now half way through _____ third term.**
    a) its b) their c) the d) it

16. The audience started to take _____ seats half an hour before the play started.
    a) their   b) its   c) theirs   d) its

17. _____ and my mother have known one another for almost forty years.
    a) She   b) Her   c) They   d) We

18. Cheer up, you two. You cannot blame _____ for the fire.
    a) yourself   b) yourselves   c) us   d) them

19. We were astonished when he gave _____ the money.
    a) us   b) I   c) it   d) she

20. She bought two bags of sweets and gave _____ to the children.
    a) them   b) it   c) all   d) little

VERBS AND PHRASAL VERBS

EXERCISE 1

Fill in the blanks using correct options.

1. Why _____ he call himself ugly?
   a) do   b) did   c) doing   d) did not

2. I think, you _____ read more books.
   a) does   b) must   c) done   d) must been

3. He _____ sitting there for three hours.
   a) has been   b) does   c) do   d) be

4. What _____ the doctor's advice to patient?
   a) were   b) are   c) is   d) am

5. Why did she _____ something so foolish?
   a) does   b) done   c) do   d) doing

6. Why _____ the man driving the bus so fast?
   a) are   b) were   c) is   d) am

7. The government _____ to provide quality healthcare to people.
   a) commit   b) committing   c) is committed   d) will committed

8. He _____ in a hurry to reach the airport.
   a) were   b) are   c) was   d) can

9. A believer smiles in public and _____ in private.
   a) wept   b) weep   c) weeping   d) weeps

10. My father _____ books to money.
    a) prefer   b) is prefer   c) prefers   d) are prefer

11. She _____ bought a dress at a very reasonable rate.
    a) been   b) am   c) does   d) has

12. Now, she _____ to be as perfect as possible.
    a) try   b) is trying   c) tried   d) are trying

13. The captain _____ present as well as the players.
    a) are   b) am   c) was   d) were

14. They _____ their friends yesterday.
    a) visits   b) visited   c) am visit   d) are visit

15. If you pass the test, then you _____ invited for the interview.
    a) is be   b) was be   c) could be   d) will be

EXERCISE 2

Complete the following sentences using correct phrasal verbs.

1. The government had to _____ from its decision.
   a) back down   b) back out   c) back up   d) pull down

2. We never thought that she would be able to _____.
   a) pull it off   b) pull it out   c) pull it about d) pull it away

3. The offer was too good to _____.
   a) pass up   b) pass out   c) pass away   d) pass on

4. Let's _____ our personal differences and work for the common good.
   a) put aside   b) put away   c) put down   d) put back

5. I don't like it when you _____ in front of your friends.
   a) put me down   b) put me off   c) put me about d) put me across

6. he couldn't _____ the feeling that he was being followed.
   a) shake at   b) shake off   c) shake down   d) shake away

7. The peon _____ and let the students into the principal's room.
   a) stood over   b) stood back   c) stood aside   d) stood under

8. The story was _____ the eighteenth century and was about two great warriors.
   a) set down   b) set around   c) set off   d) set on

9. The thug_____ with Amit's money and mobile phone.
   a) got off   b) drop off   c) took off   d) cut off

10. We were having a lovely dinner when something urgent _____ and I had to leave.
    a) came over   b) came up   c) came off   d) came around

EXERCISE 3

Fill in the correct phrasal verbs.

1. The publishers are planning to bring _____ a new edition of this book soon.
   a) in   b) forward   c) out   d) off

2. This scheme will eventually fall _____.
   a) off   b) through   c) up   d) out

3. I can't get on _____ her.
   a) at   b) with   c) by   d) after

4. I am looking _____ to being a grandmother.
   a) at   b) after   c) forward   d) up

5. When he became a celebrity he began to look down _____ his old friends.
   a) on   b) upon   c) at   d) off

6. The chief guest gave _____ the prizes.
   a) away   b) over   c) to   d) out

7. If you don't understand the meaning of a word, you should look it _____ in the dictionary.
   a) over   b) after   c) up   d) into

8. Everyone in my family looks up _____ my grandfather.
   a) to   b) at   c) down   d) after

9. The rope gave _____.
   a) away   b) way   c) up   d) in

10. We will not put _____ with such an insult.
    a) out   b) away   c) up   d) off

Adverbs and Adjectives

EXERCISE 1

Choose the appropriate adverb.

1. The soldiers fought _____ against their enemies.
   a) sadly   b) happily   c) bravely   d) busily

2. He dressed _____ for the interview.
   a) heavily   b) quietly   c) carefully   d) faithfully

3. He is _____ fat to climb up the stairs.
   a) very   b) quiet   c) too   d) so1

4. The pair of jeans is _____ tight that I can't wear it.
   a) too   b) rather   c) quite   d) so

5. _____ you have written the wrong address on the envelope.
   a) Supposedly   b) Actually   c) Probably   d) Usually

6. Most of the children gave the test _____ .
   a) confidently   b) silently   c) busily   d) kindly

7. _____ most children prefer video games.
   a) Yesterday   b) Daily   c) Formally   d) Nowadays

8. Mr Bhatt _____ comes to work in his own car.
   seldom   last year   every day   yesterday

9. The man said the train would arrive _____ .
   before   after   yesterday   soon

10. My teacher _____ scolds us in the class.
    twice   yesterday   tomorrow   hardly

27

EXERCISE 2

Fill in the blanks with correct forms of adverbs.

1. The new boy in class swims _____ than I do.
   a) fast   b) faster   c) fastest   d) fasts

2. Can you come _____ because the bus leaves at 6?
   earlier   early   earliest   earlies

3. It's very noisy. We will have to talk _____ .
   loud   more loudly   loudly   louds

4. He listened to our problems _____ than his colleagues.
   patiently   more patiently   patience   patient

5. The youngest actress acted _____ of all.
   gracefully   more gracefully   most gracefully   grace

6. We could not go any _____ as we were tired.
   far   farthest   further   more far

EXERCISE 3

Put in the correct form of adverb or adjective.

I had a (1)_____ dream last night. I was in a garden. It was getting (2)_____ and it was (3)_____ cold. My head was aching (4)_____. I was walking out of the garden when (5)_____ I saw a child sitting on a bench. He seemed very (6)_____. He looked up and smiled (7)_____ at me. I felt (8)_____ for some reason. I wanted to be (9)_____ so I tried (10)_____ to think of something to say. But I couldn't.

1. strange	stranger	strangest	strangely
2. dark	darken	darks	darkly
3. terrible	more terrible	most terrible	terribly
4. bad	very bad	more bad	badly
5. sudden	very sudden	very suddenly	suddenly
6. unhappy	unhappiness	unhappier	unhappily
7. sad	sadness	very sad	sadly
8. anxious	very anxious	more anxious	anxiously
9. friend	friends	befriend	friendly
10. hard	harder	harden	hardly

EXERCISE 4

Fill in the blanks with correct adjective order.

1. **Sonia has _____ hair.**
   a) beautiful black long
   b) beautiful long black
   c) long black beautiful
   d) black long beautiful

2. **He was wearing a _____ shirt.**
   a) dirty old green
   b) green old dirty
   c) old dirty green
   d) green dirty old

3. **All the girls fell in love with the _____ pop star.**
   a) handsome new American
   b) American new handsome
   c) new handsome American
   d) handsome American new

4. **I used to drive _____ car.**
   a) a blue old German
   b) an old German blue
   c) an old blue German
   d) blue German old

5. **He recently married a _____ woman.**
   a) young beautiful Delhi
   b) beautiful young Delhi
   b) beautiful Delhi young
   d) Delhi young beautiful

6. **This is a _____ movie.**
   a) new Bollywood wonderful
   b) wonderful Bollywood new
   c) wonderful new Bollywood
   d) Bollywood new wonderful

7. **It's in the _____ container.**
   a) large blue metal
   b) blue large metal
   c) blue metal large
   d) large metal blue

8. **He sat behind a _____ desk.**
   a) big wooden brown
   b) big brown wooden
   c) wooden big brown
   d) brown wooden big

EXERCISE 5

Circle the odd one out.

1. confine	hinder	restrict	unleash
2. correct	right	accurate	negative
3. lazy	idle	restless	lethargic
4. mean	unfriendly	unpleasant	cordial
5. joyful	mirthful	upbeat	gloomy
6. bashful	quiet	withdrawn	available

Articles and Prepositions

EXERCISE 1

Fill in the blanks with suitable articles (a, an or the).

1. What _____ shame!

2. He is _____ famous man and is known by the people.

3. I met _____ Assamese gentleman on the train.

4. If you have _____ headache you should take rest.

5. _____ union of the students has called for a strike.

6. Can you give me _____ one rupee coin?

7. _____ honest person always wins in the end.

8. She wants to buy _____ dress.

9. _____ uncle of mine from London is coming next month.

10. The train is again late by _____ hour.

11. His brother studies in _____ European university.

12. Mr. Mehta doesn't have _____ heir so his property will go to the hospital.

13. His father is _____ MP from Maharashtra.

14. _____ Shatabdi is _____ fastest train of India.

15. _____ Kosi river is known as _____ "Sorrow of Bihar".

EXERCISE 2

Fill in the blanks with suitable prepositions.

1. Who is that man standing _____ the front row of this photograph?
   a) in   b) on   c) at   d) under

2. Please put the new television _____ the corner of the sitting room.
   a) in   b) on   c) at   d) under

3. The old banyan tree _____ Bank Road has been cut down.
   a) in   b) on   c) at   d) under

4. Smita could see Nisha shedding tears as she sat _____ her.
   a) near   b) under   c) over   d) above

5. I mistook Rohan _____ Nayan because both the brothers resemble a lot.
   a) of   b) on   c) to   d) for

6. We will work overtime _____ 5:00 pm _____ 8:30 pm
   a) from, to   b) to, from   c) by, to   d) for, to

7. _____ our anniversary, we will be having a picnic.
   a) Of   b) On   c) To   d) At

8. The concert starts _____ 8:00 pm sharp so make sure you are there early.
   a) in   b) on   c) at   d) under

9. The soldier suffered minor injuries _____ the battle.
   a) within   b) during   c) of   d) at

10. They have been ordered to finish the proposal _____ a day.
    a) within   b) during   c) of   d) at

11. The teacher is very satisfied _____ my assignment. It is worthy _____ an 'A'.
    a) with, of   b) of, of   c) by, of   d) on, of

12. The boy was found guilty _____ stealing a pen from the supermarket. His parents were ashamed _____ him.
    a) of, of   b) by, by   c) on, on   d) at, at

13. We are grateful _____ the Principal for allowing us to use this classroom. However, he is rather anxious _____ the safety of the children.

   a) to, about   b) about, to   c) with, for   d) for, about

14. Studentss should not be burdened _____ too much homework. They need time _____ rest and relaxation.

   a) with, for   b) with about   c) for about   d) for, for

15. Mrs Saxena felt sorry _____ the stray dog and brought it home. However, she was worried _____ the noise the dog would make.

   a) for, about   b) by, about   c) with, for   d) to, about

Conjunctions and Punctuations

10

EXERCISE 1

Fill in the blanks with the most suitable conjunctions.

1. I went to the market _____ bought a pair of trousers.
   a) and b) but c) still d) yet

2. He _____ his father, has left for Delhi.
   a) also b) as soon as c) as well as d) yet

3. I was tired, _____ I went to the party.
   a) and b) still c) but d) so

4. The man is very rich, _____ he is unhappy.
   a) and b) so c) but d) or

5. _____ visit your aunt _____ call her up right now.
   a) Neither, nor b) Either, or c) Both, and d) Yet, still

6. He will do well in life _____ he is focused.
   a) and b) but c) still d) as

7. I was late _____ I managed to finish the work.
   a) yet b) but c) so d) and

8. I will call you _____ I reach home.
   a) if b) and c) then d) when

9. He stayed at home _____ he is ill.
   a) because b) and c) so d) but

10. Mita was late, _____ she finished the paper on time.
    a) however b) whichever c) whatever d) whenever

11. The fire brigade reached the spot _____ they could.
    a) as much as b) as well as c) as soon as d) as long as

12. I will inform you _____ I meet him.

    whenever   forever   however   ever

EXERCISE 2

Choose the sentence with the correct punctuation marks.

1. I need an intelligent sincere and committed student

    a) I need an intelligent sincere and committed student?
    b) I need an intelligent sincere and committed student.
    c) I need an intelligent, sincere and committed student.

2. I was born in kolkata but i grew up in chennai

    a) I was born in Kolkata but I grew up in Chennai.
    b) I was born in Kolkata but i grew up in Chennai
    c) I was born in Kolkata but i grew up in Chennai.

3. He asked himself, "Is this the best of all possible worlds."

    a) He asked himself, is this the best of all possible worlds?
    b) "He asked himself, is this the best of all possible worlds?"
    c) He asked himself, "Is this the best of all possible worlds?"

4. "Stopping by Woods on a Snowy Evening" is by Robert Frost, a poet from England.

    a) "Stopping By Woods on a Snowy Evening" is by Robert Frost, a poet from England.
    b) "Stopping By Woods on a Snowy Evening" is by Robert Frost, a Poet from England.
    c) Stopping by woods on a snowy evening is by Robert Frost, a poet from England.

5. I was able to find a dress, shoes, and necklace, and Rima found a shirt, pants, and sandals.

    a) I was able to find a dress shoes and necklace and Rima found a shirt pants and sandals
    b) I was able to find a dress, shoes and necklace and Rima found a shirt, pants and sandals.
    c) I was able to find a dress, shoes, and necklace. and rima found a shirt, pants, and sandals.

6. I shouted, "That hurts!".

    a) I shouted "That hurts!"
    b) I shouted, "That hurts!"
    c) I shouted, "That hurts"!

7. She said "I am going to the store"

    a) She said, "I am going to the store".
    b) She said "I am going to the store."
    c) She said, "I am going to the store."

8. **"Watch out" Raman screamed.**

    a) "Watch out!" Raman screamed.
    b) "Watch out! Raman screamed.
    c) Watch out! Raman screamed.

9. **He mumbled to himself, "could it be true? Could Mr Saxena have hidden his treasure at Golden guest house?"**

    a) He mumbled to himself, "could it be true? Could Mr saxena have hidden his treasure at Golden guest house?"
    b) He mumbled to himself, "Could it be true? Could Mr Saxena have hidden his treasure at Golden Guest House?"
    c) He mumbled to himself, "Could it be true? Could Mr Saxena have hidden his treasure at Golden Guest house?"

10. **Edwin said, that he was fine.**

    a) Edwin said "that he was fine."
    b) Edwin said that he was fine.
    c) Edwin said, "that he was fine."

11. **"I can't believe it" Meenal screamed.**

    a) "I can't believe it!" Meenal screamed.
    b) "I can't believe it! Meenal screamed.
    c) "I can't believe it!" Meenal screamed?

12. **I love to eat pizza, tacos, soda and ice cream.**

    a) I love to eat pizza, tacos, soda, and ice cream.
    b) I love to eat pizza tacos soda and ice cream.
    c) I love to eat pizza, tacos, soda, and, ice cream.

13. **Mrs Dutt is our English teacher.**

    a) Mrs Dutt is our English Teacher.
    b) Mrs Dutt is our English teacher?
    c) Mrs Dutt is our english teacher?

14. **Meenakshi felt she was prepared for the unit exam because she studied for a week before the test.**

    a) Meenakshi felt she was prepared for the unit exam, because she studied for a week before the test.
    b) Meenakshi felt she was prepared for the unit exam; because she studied for a week before the test.
    c) Meenakshi felt she was prepared for the unit exam because, she studied for a week before the test.

TENSES

EXERCISE 1

Choose the correct form of tenses to complete the sentences.

1. My mother _____ the table for dinner as soon as my father _____ home.
   a) is setting, arrived
   b) will set, arrives
   c) has set, will arrive
   d) sets, is arriving

2. The teacher _____ us on the chapter tomorrow.
   a) is questioned
   b) questions
   c) has questioned
   d) will be questioning

3. Everyone _____ that it was an accident, so you _____ me an apology.
   a) is knowing, did not owe
   b) knows, do not owe
   c) knows, are not owing
   d) knew, have not owed

4. The police _____ to solve the case but they _____ in doing so yet.
   a) are trying, did not succeed
   b) try, are not succeeding
   c) have been trying, have not succeeded
   d) try, do not succeed

5. By the time he _____ 20, he _____ a doctorate in Philosophy.
   a) is, had obtained
   b) was, had already obtained
   c) has been, has obtained
   d) was, has been obtaining

6. Nobody _____ the present if you _____ it in that suitcase.
   a) sees, are hiding
   b) has seen, hid
   c) will see, hide
   d) is seeing, have hidden

7. Be careful ! Those bowls you are carrying _____.
   a) have fallen
   b) shall fall
   c) will be falling
   d) are going to fall

8. Everyone _____ to know about it even if you do not tell them now.
   a) comes   b) will come
   c) has come   d) came

9. I _____ you for a long time. Tell me what you _____ since I last saw you.
   a) didn't see, did   b) haven't seen, have done
   c) haven't seen, have been doing d) hadn't seen, did

10. Several coconut trees _____ by lightning and some houses _____ during the heavy storm last night.
    a) were struck, have been damaged   b) had struck, damaged
    c) have been struck, have been damaged d) is struck, is damaged

11. By the end of this year, this tree _____ fruits.
    a) will bear   b) is going to bear
    c) will be bear   d) is bearing

12. I _____ to cross the road when I saw smoke rising from that house.
    a) had waited   b) was waiting
    c) had been waiting   d) has waited

13. My uncle _____ to our house tomorrow.
    a) will not be coming   b) are not going to come
    c) will not be come   d) shall not come

14. It is rude of her to behave that way. He _____ angry with her.
    a) will be   b) shall be
    c) will be being   d) has been

15. He _____ to bring the book if you do not remind him.
    a) will not be remembering   b) is not going to remember
    c) will not remember   d) shall not remember

16. My mother _____ the lunch when she gets back home.
    a) will prepare   b) is going to prepare
    c) will be preparing   d) shall be preparing

17. My father _____ us to the airport in the morning.
    a) shall drive   b) am going to drive
    c) will be driving   d) will be driven

18. You _____ better if you rest for a while and have something to eat.

    a) will feel
    b) will be feeling
    c) are going to feel
    d) shall feel

19. I _____ to Pankaj's house. I _____ back before five.

    a) will go, am going to be
    b) am going, shall be
    c) am going to go, will be
    d) will be going, am going to be

20. The airplane _____ off in a few minutes. Please fasten your seat-belts.

    a) shall take
    b) will be taken
    c) will be taking
    d) are going to take

21. We _____ on a tour round the factory tomorrow.

    a) are going to take
    b) will be taken
    c) will be taking
    d) shall take

22. The sky is covered with grey clouds. It _____ any minute now.

    a) will rain
    b) shall be raining
    c) will be rained
    d) is going to rain

23. I hope you _____ well in the examination.

    a) will be doing
    b) are going to do
    c) will be done
    d) will

24. She _____ if she continues to behave badly.

    a) will be punished
    b) is going to be punished
    c) will be punishing
    d) shall punish

25. He _____ by my house on his way to school.

    a) shall pass
    b) is going to pass
    c) will be passing
    d) will be passed

26. If we start planting the seeds now, the flowers _____ by the time mother comes back from hospital.

    a) shall bloom
    b) will be bloomed
    c) is going to bloom
    d) will be blooming

27. Can we start _____? I need to get home early tonight to make dinner.

    a) will work
    b) works
    c) working
    d) worked

28. Deepak and Amit _____ in the lift.
    a) had stuck   b) have stuck
    c) is stuck   d) are stuck

29. This _____ unbelievable! How could you betray me like this?
    a) is   b) are
    c) am   d) were

30. There is something _____ up there above the trees. Can you see it?
    a) have flown   b) flew
    c) flying   d) will fly

31. _____ you eaten breakfast? Would you like to join me?
    a) Have   b) Has
    c) Was   d) Were

32. She _____ the mayor's secretary for six years before she retired.
    a) was   b) are
    c) am   d) were

Voices and Narration

EXERCISE 1

Change the following sentences into passive voice.

1. **The boy laughed at the beggar.**

    a) The beggar was laughed by the boy.
    b) The beggar was being laughed by the boy.
    c) The beggar was being laughed at by the boy.
    d) The beggar was laughed at by the boy.

2. **The boys were playing cricket.**

    a) Cricket had been played by the boys.
    b) Cricket has been played by the boys.
    c) Cricket was played by the boys.
    d) Cricket was being played by the boys.

3. **They will demolish the entire block.**

    a) The entire block is being demolished.
    b) The block may be demolished entirely.
    c) The entire block will have to be demolished by them
    d) The entire block will be demolished.

4. **We must respect the elders.**

    a) The elders deserve respect from us.
    b) The elders must be respected.
    c) The elders must be respected by us.
    d) Respect the elders we must.

5. **We have warned you.**

    a) You have been warned.
    b) We have you warned.
    c) Warned you have been.
    d) Have you been warned.

6. Has anybody answered your question?

   a) Your question has been answered?
   b) Anybody has answered your question?
   c) Has your question been answered?
   d) Have you answered your question?

7. One must keep one's promises.

   a) One's promises are kept.
   b) Ones promises must kept.
   c) Ones promises were kept.
   d) One's promises must be kept.

8. Prepare yourself for the worst.

   a) You be prepared for the worst.
   b) The worst should be prepared by yourself.
   c) Be prepared for the worst.
   d) For the worst, preparation should be made by you.

9. He teaches us grammar.

   a) Grammar was taught to us by him.
   b) We are taught grammar by him.
   c) Grammar will be taught to us by him.
   d) We were taught grammar by him.

10. Who accomplished this major task?

   a) By whom was the major task accomplished?
   b) By who was the major task accomplished?
   c) By who was this major task accomplished?
   d) By whom was this major task accomplished?

EXERCISE 2

Fill in the blanks with suitable active and passive verb forms.

1. **This house_____ in 1970 by my grandfather.**

   a) built   b) was built   c) was build   d) has built

2. **The robbers _____ by the police.**

   a) have arrested   b) have been arrested   c) was arrested   d) had arrested

3. **We _____ for the examination.**

   a) have preparing   b) are preparing   c) had preparing   d) have been prepared

4. It _____ since yesterday.
   a) is raining   b) has been raining   c) have been raining   d) was raining

5. I _____ for five hours.
   a) have been working   b) has been working   c) was working   d) am working

6. The students _____ to submit their reports by the end of this week.
   a) have asked   b) are asked   c) has asked   d) have been asked

7. She _____ for a while.
   a) are ailing   b) is ailing   c) has been ailing   d) have been ailing

8. The teacher _____ the student for lying.
   a) has been punished   b) punished   c) is punished   d) was punished

9. I _____ to become a successful writer.
   a) have always wanted   b) am always wanted
   c) was always wanted   d) am always wanting

10. The animals in the circus _____ properly by their trainers.
    a) were not being treated   b) were not treating
    c) have not being treated   d) was not being treated

EXERCISE 3

State whether the following are active or passive.

1. The captain could not accept the team's proposals.
   active   passive

2. They have published all the details of the invention.
   passive   active

3. The new drug has not been approved for sale by the government.
   active   passive

4. Several items in the room were destroyed by the burglar.
   active   passive

5. A portrait is being painted by him.
   active   passive

42

EXERCISE 4

Change the following sentences to direct or indirect forms.

1. **Students said, "We are taking our class."**

   a) The students said that they were taking their class.
   b) The students said that they are taking their class.
   c) They students said that they have taken their class.
   d) The students said that we took our class.

2. **He said, "Are you doing your job?"**

   a) He asked me that I am doing my job.
   b) He asked me that I was doing my job.
   c) He said to me am I doing my job.
   d) He asked me whether I was doing my job.

3. **My mother says to me, "You are not hard working."**

   a) My mother told me that I am not hard working.
   b) My mother told me that I was not hard working.
   c) My mother told me that you are not hard working.
   d) My mother told me that you were not hard working.

4. **The doctor said, "A nurse will look after the patients."**

   a) The doctor said that a nurse will look after the patients.
   b) The doctor said that a nurse would look after the patients.
   c) The doctor said that a nurse will look after the patients.
   d) The doctor said a nurse would be look after the patient.

5. **He said to his father, "Please increase my pocket-money."**

   a) He requested his father to increase his pocket-money.
   b) He pleaded his father to please increase my pocket money.
   c) He told his father, "Please increase the pocket-money"
   d) He asked his father to increase his pocket-money.

6. **His father ordered him to go to his room and study.**

   a) His father shouted, "Go right now to your study room"
   b) His father said to him, "Go and study in your room."
   c) His father said firmly, "Go and study in your room."
   d) His father said, "Go to your room and study."

7. **My cousin said, "My roommate had snored throughout the night."**

   a) My cousin complained to me that his roommate is snoring throughout the night.
   b) My cousin said that his roommate snored throughout the night.
   c) My cousin told me that his roommate snored throughout the night.
   d) My cousin felt that his roommate may be snoring throughout the night.

8. **Rajat asked, "Are you going to the party tomorrow, Riya?"**

   Rajat asked whether Riya was going to the party the next day.
   Rajat asked Riya whether she was going to the party the tomorrow.
   Rajat asked Riya whether she was going to the party the next day.
   Rajat asked Riya whether you are going to the party the next day.

9. **She said that her brother was getting married**

   She said, "Her brother is getting married."
   She said, "My brother is getting married."
   She said, "My brother was getting married."
   She told, "Her brother is getting married."

10. **"What did you see in the South Pole?" Ashok asked Anil.**

    Ashok asked Anil if he saw anything in South Pole.
    Ashok asked Anil what he had seen in South Pole.
    Ashok asked Anil what did he see in South Pole.
    Ashok asked Anil that he saw anything in South Pole.

Short Composition

13

EXERCISE 1

Fill in the blanks with the most appropriate options in the notice given below.

Delhi Central School

(1) _____

(2) _____

(3) _____

To mark the Founder's Day (4)_____, the (5)_____ has decided to (6)_____ an exhibition. All badge (7)_____ are (8)_____ to attend a meeting in the school library on 11 December 2015 at 10 am to (9)_____ the (10)_____ for the exhibition.

(11)_____

(12)_____

1. message	letter	information	Notice
2. Notice	heading	date	content
3. heading	date	Notice	content
4. day	celebration	event	feast
5. class	school	college	teachers
6. arrange	start	organise	form
7. makers	holders	keepers	protectors
8. asked	told	ordered	requested
9. know	tell	say	discuss
10. creation	making	arrangements	restoration
11. date	signatory	notice	heading
12. heading	date	post	signature

45

EXERCISE 2

Fill in the blanks in the following layout of a formal letter.

1_____

_____

2_____

3_____

4_____

_____

5_____

6_____

1. a) date b) subject
   c) sender's address d) recipient's address

2. a) sender's address b) recipient's address
   c) subject d) date

3. a) recipient's address b) subject
   c) date d) none of these

4. a) content b) heading
   c) subject d) none of these

5. a) Yours faithfully b) Thank you
   c) sender's name d) none of these

6. a) recipient's address b) subject
   c) date d) name

EXERCISE 3

Read the following telephonic conversation and fill in the blanks to complete the message.

Rohan: Hello!

Naina: Yes, may I know who is calling?

Rohan: I am Rohan. May I speak to Rishav?

Naina: I am sorry. He has just gone out. I am Naina, his sister. Would you like to leave a message?

Rohan: Yes, kindly tell him that tomorrow, after school, we all are going to the International Book Fair at Pragati Maidan. If he is interested, he can join us.

Naina: Sure, I will convey your message as soon as he comes back.

Rohan: Thank you very much.

Naina: You are welcome.

Message

(1) _____

(2) _____

Dear (3) _____,

Your friend, Rohan (4) _____ to (5) _____ that (6) _____ after school, your (7) _____ will be going to the International Book Fair at Pragati Maidan and if you are also (8) _____ in going, then you can (9) _____ them.

(10) _____

1.	date	time	place	year
2.	day	time	date	year
3.	Rohan	Naina	Rishav	None
4.	was calling	called up	was calling	calling
5.	tell	understand	say	inform
6.	today	yesterday	tomorrow	later
7.	partner	Rohan	teacher	friends
8.	want	reach	arrive	interested
9.	go	come	join	reach
10.	Rohan	Rishav	Naina	Yours

Sequences–Stories, Events and Snippets

EXERCISE 1

Read the following sentences and answer the questions.

a. In 1492, King Ferdinand and Queen Isabella of Spain agreed to pay for his trip. They gave him a crew and three ships: the Nina, Pinta and Santa Maria. Columbus sailed aboard the Santa Maria.

b. The ships docked on the island of Hispaniola. Columbus named the native people he saw "Indians". In actuality, Columbus found North America, a brand new continent at that time.

c. Unfortunately, the King of Portugal refused to finance such a trip, and Columbus was forced to present his idea to the King and Queen of Spain.

d. The trip was long and hard. Many sailors grew restless and wanted to turn around. After two months at sea, land was finally sighted.

e. Christopher Columbus was born in Genoa, Italy in 1451. While spending most of his early years at sea, Columbus began to believe that he could find a shortcut to the Indies by sailing across the Atlantic Ocean.

Arrange the above sentences in logical order to form a meaningful story.

1. a-b-c-d-e   d-a-b-c-e   e-c-a-d-b   b-a-d-e-c

2. **Which country was Columbus actually looking for?**
    China   USA   Canada   India

EXERCISE 2

Read the following sentences and arrange them in a logical order.

a. People live in the same neighbourhood for many reasons.

b. To make life tolerable and bearable one must cooperate with one's neighbour.

c. It may be the nearness to one's office of work, school, hospitals and so on.

d. Living next to next is the principle of a neighbourhood. Good neighbours are what all of us want.

1.   a-b-c-d   d-a-c-b   a-c-b-d   b-a-c-d

a. Computers use tiny electrical circuits which tell it what to do.
b. Perhaps the single greatest invention of the century is the computer. It enables humans to complete tasks that may be time consuming or very repetitive in nature.
c. The difference between humans and computers is that computers work at incredible speed.
d. It achieves this by imitating human thought processes.

2.   a-b-c-d   b-a-c-d   b-d-a-c   c-d-a-b

EXERCISE 3

Read the following snippets and answer the questions that follow.

Walt Disney was initially rejected by a leading American newspaper because they found him to be not imaginative enough. Well, one can't thank that newspaper enough.

1. **What is the meaning of the word 'leading' in the above snippet?**

   a) amazing   b) fine   c) successful   d) mentoring

In a career that has spanned over 50 years, Lata Mangeshkar has sung more than thousand songs in different languages.

2. **What is the meaning of the word 'spanned' in the above snippet?**

   a) crossed   b) moved   c) extended over   d) matured

Prevention is better than cure. This holds good even in the matter of road accidents. Accidents occur due to many causes and under different circumstances.

3. **What is the meaning of the word 'spanned' in the above snippet?**

   a) precaution   b) hazard   c) fear   d) movement

Reading is the end product of writing. Unless there is something written one cannot read. So good writing is the propellant of reading.

4. **What does the word 'propellant' mean in the above snippet?**

   a) movement   b) start   c) motivation   d) agreement

Black clouds gathered above us, but we were too intent on playing football. We hoped that the clouds would go away so that we could continue playing.

5. What does the word 'intent' mean in the above snippet?

    a) nature   b) behaviour   c) reaction   d) determined

A sick man is a nuisance for himself and a nuisance for others about him. A sick person cannot go about his duties efficiently.

6. What does the word 'nuisance' mean in the above snippet?

    a) joy   b) boredom   c) rival   d) inconvenience

I believe that in this day and age when competition is rife among young people to get ahead in life, it is important to get an early start.

7. What is the meaning of the word 'rife' in the above snippet?

    a) missing   b) sweet   c) stupid   d) widespread

I am fortunate I suppose in that I am reasonably certain what I want to do with my life. I wish to be a lawyer for I believe it to be a noble and dignified profession.

8. What is meaning of the word 'reasonably' in the above snippet?

    a) little   b) theoretically   c) may be   d) quite sure

There are gadgets of recreation, like radio, television and disc and cassette players. To know the daily news and for hearing music the radio comes in handy.

9. What is the meaning of the word 'recreation' in the above snippet?

    a) remake   b) restart   c) redo   d) enjoyment

The rage of the day is television. Since it has the advantage of sound and vision it takes the place of the cinema.

10. What is the meaning of the word 'rage' in the above snippet?

    a) anger   b) wastage   c) expensive   d) highly demanded

Spoken and written expression

15

Choose the best answer for the questions given below.

1. **Your brother tells you about the party that he attended last night. Now you regret you did not go with him. What would you say?**

    a) Was the party really so amazing?
    b) I wish I had gone with you.
    c) Who all were there?
    d) Any of these

2. **Anil: Is this PVR Cinemas**

    Attendant: _____

    a) What do you think?
    b) Don't you know that?
    c) Yes, may I help you?
    d) Of course it is.

3. **Anil: Can you tell me what time is the last show?**

    Attendant: _____

    a) Its written in the brochure.
    b) Why don't you check the ticket?
    c) Come to the theatre first.
    d) One moment, please. I will check.

4. **You want to ask directions for the National Stadium. What will you say?**

    a) Where is National Stadium located?
    b) Which way leads to National Stadium
    c) Could you tell me the way to National Stadium?
    d) None of the above

5. **You are to welcome the guests for the conclave being held at your school. You will say _____**

    a) I would like to welcome you all to our school. It's a pleasure to have you here.
    b) It is good that you all came.
    c) You will find that the conclave will enlighten you.
    d) It will be a great experience

6. **Rajat: Hello**

   Ritu: May I speak to Nandini
   Rajat: _____ . Can I take a message?

   a) If you don't mind
   b) In case it is urgent
   c) I am sorry she is not at home at the moment
   d) Sorry

7. **Sneha: Let's go out for a movie**

   Atul: _____

   a) To which place?
   b) Can I take my friend?
   c) Yes, good idea!
   d) Go away!

8. **Akash: I have come first in class.**

   Arun: _____ .

   a) Did you check correctly?
   b) Good for you.
   c) That's not possible.
   d) Oh, that's great! Congratulations.

9. **Kapil goes to a garment shop to buy a shirt but the salesman is not sure whether his size is available or not. What should he say?**

   a) Try something else.
   b) You can check smaller size.
   c) I am not sure if it's available. Let me check in the store once.
   d) I am busy.

10. **Rashmi: Hi Sanjay. How are you?**

    Sanjay: _____

    a) Doesn't matter
    b) Nothing wrong with me
    c) Don't disturb
    d) Hi, I am fine, thanks. What about you?

Model Test Paper-I

Read the questions carefully and answer.

1. What is the reason of his failure in exams? (abstract noun)
   a) reason   b) in   c) exams   d) what

2. I got a C in my math test. I should _____ done better than that.
   a) have   b) had   c) has   d) did

3. _____ two rings here on my little finger belonged to _____ grandmother.
   a) These , my   b) That , mine   c) Those , me   d) The , myself

4. When the little boy grabbed the lizard, _____ tail broke off in _____ hand.
   a) it's , his   b) it , him   c) its , his   d) it , one's

5. The old woman lived alone, with _____ to look after _____.
   a) someone, her   b) anyone, herself c) everyone, she d) no one, her

Write the antonyms

6. **Compulsory**
   a) Free   b) Bound   c) Voluntary   d) Enjoyable

7. **Ridicule**
   a) Foolishness   b) Anxiety   c) Treachery   d) Praise

8. **Ancestor**
   a) Forefather   b) Descendant   c) Grandfather   d) Grandparent

9. **Coward**
   a) Valour   b) Schemer   c) Pride   d) Brave

Write the synonyms.

10. **Arrogant**
    a) Nasty   b) Typical   c) Proud   d) Rich

11. **Prompt**
    a) Alert b) Present c) Mood d) Quick

12. **sorrow**
    a) Trouble b) Misery c) Music d) Inefficient

13. **fragile**
    a) Valid b) Strong c) Delicate d) Humble

Fill in the blanks.

14. **The castle _____ in the 16th century.**
    a) built b) has built c) was built d) had built

15. **Why are you_____ by them on lunch?**
    a) take b) give c) taken d) invite

16. **The car _____ by the mechanic.**
    a) is repairing b) is being repaired c) has repaired d) has repaired

17. **Let the flowers _____.**
    a) not plucked b) not be plucked c) not be plucking d) not been plucked

18. **Finger is to hand as petal is to _____.**
    a) leaf b) tree c) plant d) flower

Undeline the odd one out.

19. Funny, Humorous, Comical, Cynical, Hilarious
20. Deceptive, Honourable, Fair, Sincere, Trustworthy
21. Thoughtful, Considerate, Amiable, Gracious, Obtuse
22. Infirm, Languid, Sluggish, Puny, Fragile, Firm

Fill in the blanks.

23. **Mayank is _____ with his friend Rahul.**
    a) picking up b) setting off c) moving in d) getting on

24. **Rajat immediately went and _____ his glass.**
    a) read out b) showed off c) filled up d) gave up

25. His class teacher never _____ on him.
   a) shut down   b) took up   c) got out   d) gave up

26. He was trying to _____ his father's shirt.
   a) put up   b) put off   c) put on   d) give up

27. The boys will visit their grandmother _____ the holidays.
   a) until   b) since   c) during   d) within

28. He got his family _____ of the burning house through the kitchen window.
   a) over   b) on to   c) out   d) away

29. What is the matter _____ you?
   a) as   b) with   c) by   d) along

30. I just got _____ the phone with the mayor.
   a) up   b) of   c) off   d) through

31. I _____ be able to give you all the information you require.
   a) need   b) should   c) used to   d) can

32. We _____ see that everything is in order before the guests arrived.
   a) must   b) have to   c) had to   d) shall

33. She _____ a scarf on her last trip to Shimla.
   a) will buy   b) bought   c) will buy   d) buys

34. She _____ the game over and over again last night until she could get a high score.
   a) is playing   b) play   c) played   d) was playing

35. We _____ going hiking this weekend.
   a) were   b) am   c) is   d) are

36. You're Shubham, the new student, _____ you?
   a) weren't   b) wasn't   c) isn't   d) aren't

37. Payal isn't 19 yet, _____ she?
   a) is   b) isn't   c) was   d) wasn't

38. Jai jogs every evening _____ he wants to lose some weight.
   a) if   b) but   c) so   d) because

39. We should eat our vegetables _____ grow tall and strong.

    a) although   b) in order to   c) but if   d) so

40. He could not see Mom _____ she came out of the hall.

    a) so that   b) in order to   c) until   d) but

Model Test Paper-2

Choose the correct answer.

Find the synonyms.

1. **Presume**
   a) Assume	b) Assure	c) Alert	d) Allow

2. **Shiver**
   a) Mend	b) Shake	c) Prepare	d) Begin

3. **Fatal**
   a) Lethal	b) Giant	c) Sweet	d) Morbid

Choose the correct antonym.

4. **Ignore**
   a) Inspect	b) Subtle	c) Deny	d) Provide

5. **Comical**
   a) Humourous	b) Jovial	c) Smooth	d) Stern

6. **Privilege**
   a) Chance	b) Independence	c) Advantage	d) Loss

Choose the word with the correct spelling.

7. a) profesional	b) economic	c) mariage	d) agains

8. a) expecct	b) aspect	c) acept	d) cureous

9. a) approach	b) prresure	c) posess	d) compas

10. a) enrgy	b) alergy	c) allergy	d) ellergy

Choose the correct option.

11. **Ending in death.**
    a) insomnia	b) fatal	c) cringe	d) hunch

12. A person who looks at the dark side of life.
  a) evident b) pessimist c) rude d) naïve

13. One who visits another country.
  a) guest b) export c) tourist d) vagabond

14. One who moves to another country.
  a) tourist b) guest c) native d) immigrant

Fill in the blanks.

15. You _____ be ashamed of yourself.
  a) could a) will c) ought to d) dare

16. We have enough chairs in here; you _____ bring in any more.
  a) must b) should c) need d) need not

17. The players _____ to come for practice if they want to beat the other team.
  a) ought b) might c) should d) could

18. The hunters _____ the tiger.
  a) could not catch b) catch c) caught d) should catch

19. After the manager _____ out the cheque, he handed it to the clerk.
  a) was writing b) writing c) wrote d) written

20. I would not have noticed her absence if you _____ it out to me.
  a) did not point b) do not point c) have not pointed d) had not pointed

Put the following sentences in order.

21. a. we celebrate Holi   b. my favourite
   c. month is   d. March when

  b-a-d-c   a-b-c-d   d-c-b-a   b-c-d-a

22. a. watch movies   b. did we have
   c. the chance to   d. seldom

  d-b-c-a   a-b-c-d   c-a-b-d   d-c-a-b

Fill in the blanks.

23. Dr. Swami comes from either Oxford or Cambridge, I can't remember _____ .
    a) what   b) where   c) which   d) that

24. Why do you want a new job _____ you've got such a good one already?
    a) that   b) where   c) which   d) when

25. We couldn't buy anything because _____ of the shops were open.
    a) all   b) no one   c) none   d) nothing

26. I asked two people the way to the station but _____ of them knew.
    a) none   b) either   c) both   d) neither

27. The cadets saluted the _____ .
    a) plumber   b) party   c) bodyguard   d) admiral

28. On the plane, the _____ made sure that all the passengers fastened their seatbelts.
    a) stewardess   b) pilot   c) umpire   d) waitress

29. It's a difficult decision for the _____ .
    a) admiral   b) player   c) pilot   d) umpire

30. Go to the _____ and get these medicines quickly.
    a) pharmacist   b) greengrocer c) tailor   d) shopkeeper

31. Are you sure that book is not _____? It has your name on it.
    a) theirs   b) yours   c) its   d) ours

32. Today's sweet corn is not _____ last week's.
    a) as tasty as b) tasty   c) tastier   d) tastiest

33. The door creaked loudly _____ she closed it.
    a) unless   b) in order to c) although   d) as

34. You and _____ can be partners. We can sit together in class.
    a) him   b) me   c) I   d) her

35. _____ what happened, you are still my friend.
    a) Even though b) Despite   c) Until   d) Since

Find the odd one out.

36. **graceful**
    elegant awkward decent

37. **admit**
    accept acknowledge deny

38. **command**
    order impose petition

39. **sinful**
    bad blessed ruthless

40. **dazzle**
    gloom lustre shine

Model Test Paper-3

Choose the correct answers.

1. I will be ready to leave _____ 10 minutes.
   a) above b) on c) in d) under

2. The child responded to his mother's demands _____ throwing tantrums.
   a) with b) by c) from d) of

3. I will wait _____ 6:30, but then I'm going home.
   a) at b) until c) from d) by

4. The police caught the thief _____ the corner of the street.
   a) in b) at c) for d) of

Change to indirect speech.

5. The new student asked the old one, "Do you know my name?"
   a) The new student asked the old one did he know his name.
   b) The new student asked the old one if he knew his name.
   c) The new student asked the old one that whether he knew his name.
   d) The new student asked the old one if he knows his name.

6. I said to my friend, "Good morning. Let us go for a picnic today."
   a) I wished my friend good morning and proposed that we should go for a picnic that day.
   b) I wish my friend good morning and proposed that they should go for a picnic that day.
   c) I told good morning to my friend and asked to go for a picnic that day.
   d) I told good morning to my friend and suggested to go for a picnic today.

7. I said to my mother, "I will certainly take you to Bangalore this week."
   a) I told my mother he would certainly take her to Bangalore that week.
   b) I told my mother that I would certainly take her to Bangalore that week.
   c) I told my mother that she would certainly take her to Bangalore that week.
   d) I told to my mother that I would take you to Bangalore that week.

Change to direct speech.

8. He said he goes for a walk every morning.
   a) He said, "I go for a walk every morning."
   b) He said, "I am go for a walk every morning."

c) He said, "I went for a walk every morning."
   d) He said, "I goes for a walk every morning."

9. **The Prime Minister said that no one would be allowed to disturb the peace.**
   a) The Prime Minister said, "No one can disturb the peace."
   b) The Prime Minister said, "We shall not allow anyone to disturb the peace."
   c) The Prime Minister said, "No one will disturb the peace."
   d) The Prime Minister said, "We would not allow no one to disturb the peace."

Choose the correct answer.

10. **She didn't come to school today, _____ she?**
    don't   didn't   does   did

11. **She has been to the doctor to check her injured knee, _____ she?**
    hasn't   have   has   haven't

12. **He does have a test tomorrow morning, _____ he?**
    hadn't   haven't   don't   doesn't

13. **I just _____ that I have something important to tell you.**
    had remembered   remembered   were remembering   is remembering

14. **Ankush and Ayush _____ identical twins.**
    are   is   was   has

15. **Nalini _____ to the scarf store to find a red scarf to match her red hat.**
    go   went   gone   is going

16. **He is still a very handsome man _____ turning 61 today.**
    because   unless   despite   but

17. **Can you do something _____ this broken jar?**
    off   with   on   in

18. **This _____ the last time I get to watch a movie here.**
    will be   been   be   being

19. **Tanya _____ reads a book when she is tired of practising on her piano.**
    sometimes   hardly   never   seldom

20. **Can you get me a _____ cloth for wiping the mirror?**
    drier   as dry as   driest   dry

21. **Sukanya irons her school uniform _____ before she goes to bed.**
    a) themselves   b) herself   c) himself   d) myself

22. **You _____ be right, but I would still like to check.**
    a) may   b) can   c) should   d) must

23. **_____ you turn down the volume, please?**
    a) Can   b) May   c) If   d) But

24. **Who can it be? It _____ be the postman.**
    a) may not   b) can't   c) must not   d) shouldn't be

25. **The weather _____ be hotter tomorrow.**
    a) is   b) may   c) can't   d) must

26. **I _____ college last year.**
    a) left   b) was leaving   c) has left   d) am leaving

27. **The light _____ out while I was reading.**
    a) went   b) goes   c) go   d) came

28. **The light always _____ out when I am about to study.**
    a) go   b) goes   c) has gone   d) gone

29. **She _____ the piano when I met her.**
    a) was playing   b) played   c) has played   d) is playing

30. **The train _____.**
    a) has just left   b) had just left   c) is just left   d) would just left

31. **James is honest _____ industrious.**
    a) but   b) as well as   c) so   d) while

32. **He neither respects his aged parents _____ helps them financially.**
    a) nor   b) or   c) either   d) but

33. **_____ did I reach the station than the train left.**
    a) No sooner   b) As soon as   c) Nearly   d) Finally

34. **I _____ love and respect my parents.**
    a) both   b) so   c) together   d) along

35. I don't know _____ I will be able to come or not.
    a) whether   b) so   c) when   d) how

36. We need someone with _____ knowledge of German.
    a) excellent   b) an excellent   c) the excellent   d) a excellent

37. She has _____ understanding of the subject.
    a) thorough   b) a thorough   c) the thorough   d) thoroughly

38. She's in _____ health.
    a) good   b) a good   c) the good   d) all good

39. Professionals _____ teachers and lawyers should have good communication skills.
    a) such like   b) such as   c) as   d) as such

40. She asked him why _____ late.
    a) he was   b) was he   c) he would   d) would he

Model Test Paper-4

Answer the following questions correctly.

1. She applauded him _____ that he had done well.
   a) said   b) saying   c) say   d) says

2. She _____ to prefer strawberries.
   a) like   b) likes   c) liking   d) will liking

3. She challenged him that he _____ run five miles without stopping.
   a) could not   b) cannot   c) will   d) cannot be

4. _____ you like to have a cup of tea?
   a) Cannot   b) Might   c) Will be   d) Would

Choose the correct synonym.

5. **Dismayed**
   a) Confused   b) Scared   c) Worried   d) Frightened

6. **Pail**
   a) Pocket   b) Shoe   c) Shovel   d) Bucket

7. **Culminate**
   a) Discourage   b) Mislead   c) Conclude   d) Corrupt

Choose the correct antonym.

8. **Dissuade**
   a) Discourage   b) Fool   c) Negate   d) Persuade

9. **Eradicate**
   a) Uproot   b) Instill   c) Mislead   d) Terminate

10. **Inflammable**
    a) Excitable   b) Hot   c) Calm   d) Irritate

11. **Prominent**
    a) Obscure   b) Apparent   c) Visible   d) Noticeable

Change from active to passive voice.

12. Please keep quiet.
    a) You are told for keep quiet.
    b) You are requested to keep quiet.
    c) You are requested for keep quiet.
    d) You are told to keep quiet.

13. Who is creating this mess?
    a) By whom this mess is being created?
    b) By whom is this mess being created?
    c) Who has been created this mess?
    d) By whom has this mess been created?

14. He asked me what my post was.
    a) I get asked what my post was.
    b) I could asked what my post was.
    c) I was asked what my post was.
    d) I had asked what my post was.

Change from passive to active.

15. The student was found to be guilty by him.
    a) He found the student guilty.
    b) He find the student guilty.
    c) The student is guilty by him.
    d) He called the student guilty.

16. His hard work satisfied me.
    a) I was satisfied for his hard work.
    b) I was satisfied by his hard work.
    c) I was satisfied with his hard work.
    d) I was satisfied at his hard work.

Choose the correct meaning.

17. Imminent
    a) Impure   b) Upcoming   c) Proud   d) Unsteady

18. Restive
    a) At rest   b) In motion   c) Relay   d) Uneasy

19. Ravage
    a) Ruin   b) Annoy   c) To move back   d) Popular

20. **Surmount**

    a) Overcome   b) Defeated   c) Wait   d) Hurry

Choose the correct answer.

21. **I wonder what _____ they do in next class.**
    a) will   b) did   c) does   d) could

22. **We _____ be waiting for them.**
    a) would   b) will be   c) shall   d) could

23. **You should _____ be confident of your success.**
    a) been   b) being   c) be   d) may

24. **Something _____ to be done about it.**
    a) should   b) ought   c) must   d) should

25. **She wasn't _____ impressed with the results.**
    a) quiet   b) quite   c) quiets   d) quietly

26. **You are late. _____ you can try if you wish.**
    a) Wherever   b) Whatsoever   c) However   d) Whenever

27. **Wise men seek knowledge _____ the ignorant shun it.**
    a) when   b) so   c) but   d) whereas

28. **The moment _____ is lost is lost forever.**
    a) if   b) that   c) but   d) when

29. **They sent for the doctor _____ came at once.**
    a) who   b) which   c) whom   d) that

30. **There was a silence _____ the guests had gone.**
    a) when   b) where   c) before   d) after

31. **She began to cry _____ she had lost her golden chain.**
    a) when   b) as   c) till   d) because

32. **She will not come _____ we compel her.**
    a) if   b) till   c) unless   d) until

33. Mr Khan was always angry _____ his juniors.

　a) with　　b) by　　c) to　　d) on

34. He started shouting _____ his younger brother.

　a) on　　b) at　　c) by　　d) for

35. They stayed away _____ him as much as possible.

　a) to　　b) by　　c) of　　d) from

36. My father has been serving in the army _____ 20 years.

　a) by　　b) from　　c) since　　d) for

37. He has been suffering from fever _____ Monday.

　a) for　　b) since　　c) with　　d) by

38. This is the building. It is going to be demolished.

　a) This is the building that is going to be demolished.
　b) This is the building and is going to be demolished.
　c) This is the building it is going to be demolished.
　d) This is the building which is going to be demolished.

39. I know a man. The man wears artificial legs.

　a) I know a man he wears artificial legs.
　b) I know a man it wears artificial legs.
　c) I know a man who wears artificial legs.
　d) I know a man whom wears artificial legs.

40. He is the man. His son recently moved to USA for studies.

　a) He is the man that son recently moved to USA for studies.
　b) He is the man which son recently moved to USA for studies.
　c) He is the man whose son recently moved to USA for studies.
　d) He is the man whom son recently moved to USA for studies.

Model Test Paper-5

Choose the correct answers.

1. **Raining cats and dogs**
   a) drizzling slightly
   b) raining very heavily
   c) threatening to rain shortly
   d) the thunder and lightning that scare the animals

2. **Just a stone's throw away**
   a) a great distance
   b) in the same house
   c) in the next town
   d) a very short distance

3. **Pep me up**
   a) put me to sleep
   b) make me feel better
   c) give me a good food
   d) let me dance

4. **Fell on deaf ears**
   a) caused great sorrow
   b) could not be understood
   c) went unnoticed
   d) could not be heard

Choose the correct meanings of the following words.

5. **Veer**
   a) Great courage   b) Shoot   c) Shift   d) Pride

6. **Untoward**
   a) Peaceful   b) Retrace   c) Rebate   d) Troublesome

7. **Turbulent**
   a) Unstable   b) Proud   c) Abuse   d) Wicked

8. **Remonstrate**
   a) Defeat   b) Familiar   c) Protest   d) Approve

Choose the correct answer.

9. Nobody told us to set off and we _____ behind.
   a) left b) were left c) were leaving d) had left

10. The pots and pans seem to _____.
    a) have been cleaned b) be cleaning c) have cleaned d) have been cleaning

11. The pictures _____ on my trip to London last month.
    a) had taken b) were taking c) have taken d) were taken

12. We _____ by him before so we no longer trust him.
    a) have tricked b) have been tricked c) are tricked d) are being tricked

13. I always have trouble _____ phone numbers.
    a) to remember b) remembering c) remember d) to remembering

14. It _____ for six hours.
    a) has been raining b) is raining c) was raining d) had been raining

15. Sorry I broke the glass; I _____ help it.
    a) couldn't b) couldn't have c) couldn't but d) can't

16. _____ his best efforts, he could not pass the test.
    a) In spite of b) Because of c) Although d) Since

17. _____ he hadn't paid the fee, they cancelled his subscription.
    a) Since b) So c) If d) Although

18. If I _____ enough time tomorrow, I will come and see you.
    a) have b) will have c) should have d) could have

19. I would get up earlier if there _____ a good reason to.
    a) is b) was c) would d) were

20. This time tomorrow I _____ on my bed.
    a) will lie b) will be lying c) lying d) would lie

21. Have you ever watched _____ a rainbow appears after the rain?
    a) how b) the way c) about d) as

22. The old man _____ in the middle of his speech.
   a) broke up b) broke in c) broke down d) broke off

23. Could you _____ the candle?
   a) blow off b) blow on c) blow out d) blow up

24. The factory workers have _____ the strike.
   a) called off b) called on c) called at d) called in

25. The policeman tried to _____ information from the robber.
   a) call off b) call forth c) call out d) call up

26. English _____ all over the world.
   a) speaks b) has spoken c) is spoken d) spoken

27. The news _____.
   a) has confirmed b) has been confirmed
   c) confirmed d) confirm

28. _____ Dalhousie is the cheapest.
   a) Of all hill stations b) From all hill stations
   c) To all hill stations d) By all hill stations

29. He came to meet me _____.
   a) at 5 o'clock b) in 5 o'clock c) on 5 o'clock d) to 5 o'clock

30. He is very good _____.
   a) in drawing b) at drawing c) to drawing d) on drawing

31. The train was moving _____.
   a) fully speed b) at full speed c) in full speed d) on full speed

32. Most of the people said that they _____ anyone cross the river in this weather.
   a) had never known b) never knew
   c) had never been known d) have never known

33. If you had asked me, I _____ you with pleasure.
   a) would help b) would have helped
   c) had helped d) would have been helped

34. I was going to have lunch when they _____ me.
   a) had called   b) called   c) were called   d) were calling

35. No one could explain how the prisoner _____ from the prison.
   a) had escaped   b) has escaped   c) had been escaped   d) was escaped

Fill in the blanks correctly.

India (36)_____ with many historical places and monuments. Agra (37)_____ an important place amongst them. The famous Taj Mahal (38)_____ this city. It was my long (39)_____ dream to visit Taj Mahal and it (40)_____ last month when the school organised a trip to Agra.

36.	stud	is stud	studded	is studded
37.	occupy	occupying	is occupying	occupies
38.	immortal	immortalised	is immortalised	has immortalised
39.	cherish	cherishable	cherished	cherishing
40.	was fulfilled	fulfilled	fulfilling	was fulfil

Answer Key

Chapter 1

Exercise 1

1. a	2. b	3. b	4. a
5. c	6. b	7. a	8. d
9. c	10. b	11. d	12. d
13. d	14. a	15. c	16. a
17. c	18. b	19. a	20. c
21. d	22. a	23. c	24. d
25. d	26. d	27. c	28. c
29. c	30. b	31. a	32. d
33. b	34. c	35. c	

Chapter 2

Exercise 1

1. a	2. d	3. d	4. d
5. b	6. c	7. c	8. a
9. c	10. b	11. b	12. d
13. b	14. d	15. c	16. d
17. a	18. d	19. d	20. d
21. b	22. d	23. b	24. d
25. a	26. d	27. d	28. a
29. d	30. c	31. d	32. a
33. b	34. d	35. d	

Chapter 3

Exercise 1

1. d	2. d	3. d	4. b
5. d	6. d	7. c	8. a
9. d	10. d	11. a	12. c
13. a	14. b	15. d	16. b

Exercise 2

1. a	2. a	3. a	4. c
5. a	6. b	7. a	8. c
9. b	10. c	11. d	12. c

Exercise 3

1. b	2. d	3. d	4. d
5. c	6. b	7. d	8. c
9. b	10. b	11. b	12. d

Chapter 4
Exercise 1

1. d	2. a	3. c	4. a
5. c	6. b	7. d	8. d
9. d	10. b	11. d	12. a
13. c	14. d	15. a	

Exercise 2

1. c	2. d	3. b	4. a
5. c	6. d	7. a	8. d
9. c	10. c	11. d	12. b

Exercise 3

| 1. d | 2. b | 3. a | 4. d |
| 5. b | 6. b | 7. c | |

Chapter 5
Exercise 1

1. b	2. c	3. b	4. d
5. a	6. c	7. d	8. b
9. a	10. b	11. d	12. b
13. d	14. d	15. b	16. a
17. c	18. b	19. a	20. d
21. b	22. c		

Exercise 2

| 1. a-d-c-b | 2. c-d-b-a | 3. c-d-a-b | 4. b-a-c-d |
| 5. d-a-c-b | 6. c-b-a-d | 7. b-a-d-c | 8. d-b-c-a |

Chapter 6
Exercise 1

| 1. d | 2. c | 3. a | 4. a |
| 5. d | 6. c | 7. d | 8. c |

Exercise 2

| 1. b | 2. a | 3. c | 4. a |
| 5. c | 6. c | 7. d | 8. d |

Exercise 3

| 1. c | 2. a | 3. c | 4. c |
| 5. d | | | |

Exercise 4

1. c	2. d	3. a	4. d
5. d	6. d	7. b	8. a
9. b	10. a	11. c	12. d
13. c	14. d	15. a	16. b
17. a	18. b	19. a	20. a

Chapter 7
Exercise 1

1. c	2. b	3. a	4. c
5. c	6. c	7. c	8. c
9. d	10. c	11. d	12. b
13. c	14. b	15. d	

Exercise 2

1. a	2. a	3. a	4. a
5. a	6. b	7. b	8. b
9. c	10. b		

Exercise 3

1. c	2. b	3. b	4. c
5. b	6. a	7. c	8. a
9. b	10. c		

Chapter 8
Exercise 1

1. c	2. c	3. c	4. d
5. c	6. a	7. d	8. a
9. d	10. d		

Exercise 2

1. b	2. b	3. c	4. b
5. c	6. c		

Exercise 3

1. strange	2. dark	3. terribly	4. badly
5. suddenly	6. unhappy	7. sadly	8. anxious
9. friendly	10. hard		

Exercise 4

1. b	2. a	3. a	4. c
5. b	6. c	7. a	8. b

Exercise 5

1. unleash	2. negative	3. restless	4. cordial
5. gloomy	6. available		

Chapter 9
Exercise 1

1. a	2. a	3. an	4. a
5. The	6. a	7. An	8. a
9. An	10. an	11. a	12. an
13. an	14. The, the	15. The, the	

Exercise 2

1. a	2. a	3. c	4. a
5. d	6. a	7. b	8. c
9. b	10. a	11. a	12. a
13. a	14. a	15. a	

Chapter 10
Exercise 1

1. a	2. c	3. b	4. c
5. b	6. d	7. b	8. c
9. a	10. a	11. c	12. a

Exercise 2

1. c	2. a	3. c	4. a
5. b	6. b	7. c	8. a
9. b	10. b	11. a	12. a
13. a	14. a		

Chapter 11
Exercise 1

1. b	2. d	3. b	4. c
5. b	6. c	7. d	8. b
9. c	10. a	11. b	12. b
13. a	14. a	15. c	16. a
17. c	18. a	19. c	20. c
21. b	22. a	23. a	24. a

25. c	26. a	27. c	28. d
29. a	30. c	31. a	32. a

Chapter 12
Exercise 1

1. d	2. d	3. c	4. c
5. a	6. c	7. d	8. c
9. b	10. d		

Exercise 2

1. b	2. b	3. b	4. b
5. a	6. d	7. c	8. b
9. a	10. a		

Exercise 3

1. active	2. active	3. passive	4. passive
5. passive			

Exercise 4

1. a	2. d	3. b	4. b
5. a	6. d	7. c	8. c
9. b	10. b		

Chapter 13
Exercise 1

1. Notice	2. date	3. heading	4. celebration
5. school	6. organise	7. holders	8. requested
9. discuss	10. arrangements	11. signature	12. post

Exercise 2

1. recipient's address
2. date
3. subject

4.	content
5.	Yours faithfully
6.	name

Exercise 3

1. date	2. day	3. Rishav	4. called up
5. inform	6. tomorrow	7. friends	8. interested
9. join	10. Naina		

Chapter 14
Exercise 1

1. e-c-a-d-b   2. India

Exercise 2

1. d-a-c-b   2. b-a-c-d

Exercise 3

1. c	2. c	3. a	4. c
5. d	6. d	7. d	8. d
9. d	10. d		

Chapter 15
Exercise 1

1. b	2. c	3. d	4. c
5. a	6. c	7. c	8. d
9. c	10. d		

Model Test Paper 1

1. a 2. a 3. a 4. c 5. d 6. c 7. d 8. b 9. d 10. c 11. d 12. b 13. c 14. c 15. c 16. b 17. b 18. d 19. Cynical 20. Deceptive 21. Obtuse 22. Firm 23. c 24. c 25. d 26. c 27. c 28. c 29. b 30. c 31. d 32. a 33. b 34. c 35. d 36. d 37. a 38. d 39. b 40. c

Model Test Paper 2

1. a 2. b 3. a 4. a 5. d 6. d 7. b 8. b 9. a 10. c 11. b 12. b 13. c 14. d 15. c 16. d 17. a 18. a 19. c 20. d 21. b-c-d-a 22. d-b-c-a 23. c 24. d 25. c 26. d 27. d 28. a 29. d 30. a 31. b 32. a 33. d 34. c 35. b 36. awkward 37. deny 38. petition 39. blessed 40. gloom

Model Test Paper 3

1. c 2. b 3. b 4. b 5. b 6. a 7. b 8. a 9. b 10. d 11. a 12. d 13. b 14. a 5. b 16. c 17. b 18. a 19. a 20. d 21. b 22. a 23. a 24. b 25. b 26. a 27. a 28. b 29. a 30. a 31. b 32. a 33. a 34. a 35. a 36. b 37. b 38. a 39. b 40. a

Model Test Paper 4

1. b 2. b 3. a 4. d 5. c 6. d 7. c 8. d 9. b 10. c 11. a 12. b 13. b 14. c 15. a 16. c 17. b 18. d 19. a 20. a 21. a 22. c 23. c 24. b 25. a 26. c 27. d 28. b 29. a 30. d 31. d 32. c 33. a 34. b 35. d 36. d 37. b 38. d 39. c 40. c

Model Test Paper 5

1. b 2. d 3. b 4. c 5. c 6. d 7. a 8. c 9. b 10. a 11. d 12. b 13. b 14. a 15. a 16. a 17. a 18. a 19. b 20. b 21. b 22. c 23. c 24. a 25. b 26. c 27. b 28. a 29. a 30. b 31. b 32. a 33. b 34. b 35. a 36. is studded 37. occupies 38. has immortalised 39. cherished 40. was fulfilled